Scent of Love

Teresa E. Gallion

inner child press, ltd.

Credits

Author

Teresa E. Gallion

Editor

Debbi Brody

Cover Graphics

Denise Weaver Ross

Back Cover Photo

Dee Cohen Bruno

Cover Design

inner child press, ltd.

General Information
Scent of Love
Teresa E. Gallion

1st Edition: 2020

Publisher Information:
Inner Child Press International
www.innerchildpress.com

ISBN-13: 978-1-952081-32-3 (inner child press, ltd.)

$ 17.95

Dedication

To

All Seekers of Love
Through Time

And
to the Memory
of my Beloved Mother

Teresa Lewis Gallion

How do I love thee
Let me count the ways

Elizabeth Barrett Browning

Table of Contents

Scent of Love

Table of Contents . . . *continued*

Table of Contents . . . *continued*

Love in the Middle of Grief   57

Love in the Fields of Awakening   69

Table of Contents . . . *continued*

Acknowledgements

Grateful acknowledgement is made to the following Anthologies in which half of the poems in this collection first appeared.

Year of the Poet Monthly Anthologies 2014 through 2020
The Poetry Posse: An Anthology of Love
Wisdom Shares, Legends and Monsters: A Jules Poetry Playhouse Project Anthology
Confidence, House of Cards: Ekphrastic Poetry Anthology, a Jules Poetry Playhouse Project Based on the Art of Denise Weaver Ross

A special thank you to Debbi Brody who always keeps me grounded during the review and editing process with honest tough love.
Light and love to you my friend.

A special thank you to Mary Dezember whose powerful verse in her book, *Earth-Marked Like You*, motivated me to finish this body of work.
Light and love to you my friend.

A special thank you to Denise Weaver Ross who patiently educated and walked me through the process of developing the book cover art.
Light and Love to you my friend.

I lay a prayer on your chest
To soothe your burning sleep
It is selfish to hold back
When love flows in my river

Teresa E. Gallion

Preface

The Scent of Love is everywhere throughout our lives. Sometimes we do not notice because we sleepwalk through life. Some of us wake up and the heavy burden of earth teases us with scents everywhere. Then there are those of us who rise above earth to experience divine love and ecstasy. We are all on a journey at different places along love's highway. And that is okay.

A part of the seeker's life is invested in longings that start in the physical, expands in the mental, faces the storms in the emotional and arrives at the spiritual ready to merge in the ultimate experience of divine love in this life time.

A poet forages in the shifting valleys of love in harmony and conflict with mind, body and soul. The poems in this body of work address the desire to reach for the union of mind, body and soul in a spiritual merger.

Love is universal and there is something for everyone between the sheets of these lines.

May you be intimately touched at every level you are ready to receive.

May you be stimulated physically, emotionally and spiritually as you move through love's perpetual garden of scents and find the scent of love that resonates and lifts your soul.

Teresa E. Gallion
Light and Love
September 2020

Scent of Love

Teresa E. Gallion

Burning in the fire of love
We surrender to the moment
Spirit offers a ride
We fly on the wings of butterflies

Teresa E. Gallion

Love
Riding the Rapids

The stroke of my pen
Is like a wander hussy
Trying to find herself
In love everywhere

Teresa E. Gallion

Scent of Love

You look at me
and penetrate my heart.
Now I am a prisoner
of your words teasing me
at every level of my being.

My thoughts are obsessed
with the idea of your love.
I undress in my dreams
and fall into your embrace.
When I wake up I stroke
the image rubbing my heart.

I ache for your presence
to touch on the earth plane.
Then sadness bursts my
chest wide open, floods
my body with the water of pain.
You will not see this nor feel this.
You are only in my mind.

As the warmth of you
fades into morning,
reality sucks my blood.
I cry alone in the physical
totally protected
by sacred fragrances.

I want to go back to my dreams
where my soul may engage
the everlasting scent.
So I close my eyes,
embraced in spiritual light
and awaken to the scent of love.

What We Need

Our souls already know each other.
When I think of you, my heart flutters
and I long for you beside me.

When I look into your eyes,
I melt like snow
into our pool of desire.

When I hear your voice,
I can barely breathe
from an overflow of our joy.

We echo the same love notes
that need release
to the universe.

There is just one thing left to do.
Explore our bodies in new light
since we have learned so much
from many past lives apart.

Teresa E. Gallion

Let Soul Fly

Today I sit with the Beloved
in need of a spiritual massage.
My world is spinning like a dervish
giving me an unwelcome headache.

The rain pleasures my windows
with furious strokes of love.
The desert howls with joy
for the gift of water.

The energy surrounding me
makes me high.
I want to run outside and hug somebody.

The Beloved touches my hand softly.
Tells me to breathe in, breathe out
to calm my excited soul
and send monkey mind to bed.

The new unfoldment is coming.
You must be still and
listen to the sound and hug the light.
This sacred union brings greater love.

The sparrow sings to the heart.
Let the soul fly unadorned.

Merging

The full orchestra of my heart
plays for you
sitting here in the river.
What bliss is this sound of water
flowing from your lips crushing me.
The water rolls over my feet
like a melody from your touch.

I want to cuddle you here
in this river now, merge with the water,
bind my thighs to yours, swim
in the reflecting pool of your body
and feel your presence all over me.

Wrap me in your bosom
and when I look up,
your eyes make love to my essence
causing an orgasm from my delicate flower.

I want to hold on to you and swim to nirvana,
emerge naked, wet as one in eternity
because I surrender to your love.

Broken Pieces

You are having feelings
never experienced before.
You feel excitement and
tension that burns your thighs.

Your mind cannot engage
nor label what the body is feeling.
Is it possible or can it be
a suppressed desire
to try an alternative love.

You dig deeper into your work
to avoid the pleas deep within you.
You close your legs
in fear of possibilities.

But the pull on your heart
is falling in broken pieces
beside your bed.

Piercing

You ask, what are your motives?

I want to pierce your heart
with love stains, take you
to the woods and introduce
you to the Beloved.

You ask, how is my life?

It is grateful, joyful
on my journey home.
It is missing your presence,
the energy I need to walk
daily supported by the touch
of your soul.

You ask, how do we begin?

The tapestry of love unfolds
individually and collectively
between our souls.
I feel you at every level
of my beingness.
No rules may restrict love
that is purely from the heart.

Love Chasing the Broken

You are a spiritual essence
cruising through back alleys
to touch loss souls with baggage.
Those that dare to let go
find life's weight lighter.

Your tongue is sharp.
A weak mind bends to your will.
They try to run on legs that buckle
under the heat of verbs that cut
like a two-edge sword.

You baptize their hands with pure blood
and when they wrap them around love,
they rise into the arms of Spirit.

Forbidden Fruit

I read down your bones caressing earth
leaving a trail of agony.
I try to follow the forbidden
and water the terrain with tears

unjustified with selfish desire.
A dry warning follows me
that says *let it go.*
You must burn alone.

Desires of the flesh may deceive.
Stubborn resistance presses my chest.
I crave your touch beyond reason.

My Spirit Guide opens a window of light,
shows protective angels throwing
ropes at the mountain.

The message says let go, let go
as I hold you in the twin flames of love.

Clipped Wings

A prayer to her feet
makes her toes dance.
She wants to leap from this mountain
and float on the wings of love.

The Beloved says no.
You still have work today
on the earth plane.
No whining or weeping.

Just be in your moment,
open your eyes and
see for the first time
the magnificence of your soul.

She opens her arms to the sky.
They feel like angel wings.
The Beloved clips each one.

Clouds of a Woman

The cloud kissed the mountain.
He sucked her in until
her moisture wet his face.

Now she had his attention.
She moved and caressed him
until his juices flooded his side.

The Sun broke him down.
His lust flooded the valley
a thousand feet below.

The grass ladies screamed all day
teased by the cloud's moisture,
ignored his flood tide.

The powerful clouds of a woman
may take whatever pleases her
in the meadows of love.

Please Hug Me

She sleeps in a bed of holiness
as I move my pen in the sacred meadow
waiting for the sunset's grace.

I miss you sitting next to me
and long for your touch
so we may exhale together
to feel the love of spirit.

You sometimes bless my morning
with a whisper in the wind
that says, *Hi! I'm doing well. Are you?*
Puts a smile on my face.

That soft voice sends shivers to my heart.
Please hug me so I may know
the true meaning of love.

Spiritual Womb

She invites you to her womb
and you eagerly accept.
You drink her into ecstasy
as the ancient howl
from her throat brings out
the tender beast in you.

She knows in her womb
you hold the magic of bliss.
Your thoughts penetrate her
and the water of ecstasy
rolls down her thighs.

Then you kill hope and her eyes swell.
She squeezes her heart muscle,
imagines you back into happiness.
Hope caresses the smile
coming back to your face.

The Beloved smiles with approval
for two loves in his care.
The possibility of you suffering
is an unacceptable cookie to taste.

Undress Me

You undress my soul
through the scan of blue-green eyes.
I dare not hold you close to my heart.
I know the burning in my chest is holy
and painful when lack of experience
comes to the healing temples.

My soul saw you in the temple of desire.
Your light body scorched my essence
as you floated away from me.
I was unable to follow you
because I had not passed
all my learning rituals. The forbidden
grip held onto my light body.

The boat bound for earth
had one seat left. I sold my
soul to the body to run away
from home.

I Wanted to Tell You

I wanted to tell you.
My touch is holy
and my embrace is sacred.
When could I tell you
and you truly hear me.

I wanted to tell you.
I have eagle eyes.
I see beyond your breast
the scar that holds your fear.
I have the power to heal.

I wanted to tell you.
the flow from your womb
is righteous.
When could I tell you
and you truly feel me.

I wanted to tell you.
Your heart is a ball of purity
in a sea of emotions.
Those emotions crippling you,
I have the power to remove.

I wanted to tell you.
I carry the love of spirit
on my shoulders.
When could I tell you
and you truly believe.

I wanted to tell you.
I hold the spark of divine love
and want to share it with you.
I am capable of surrender
I have the power to give.

Teresa E. Gallion

Friends

Come to my house friend
when you feel the need
for a healing massage.

My doors are wide open.
There is a trail of roses
to my door kept for friends.
So come anytime
the spirit moves you.

My soul sits quietly with the Beloved
in the garden of love with space
reserved for friends.

Back to the Spirit

I dare you to come out to play,
frolic in the water of purity
and feel the light of Spirit
on your face.

I challenge you to taste love
in the black sand.
It is sacred and pure.
You listen but you do not hear me.

I invite you to take the risk
to connect with the love stream
on an ecstatic ride
back to the heart of spirit.

Everlasting Love

Every morning I wake up,
I fall in love with you again.
Our love is forever.

When you are in my arms,
I want to stay forever
in your presence.

When we reach the edge of earth,
I want to hold your hands, leap
to the first step on the heavenly planes.

I want to begin that exciting journey
with you
of everlasting love.

Reality Check

He thinks he knows the color of my thighs
based on his experience with the nectar of
loose women.

His ego is a generalization of reality,
masculine in its bias and loss
in the presence of the feminine.

There is much to be learned about him
once passions fruits are no longer ripe
and he sheds all his boyish baggage.

Then we can begin a true engagement
to explore the thirst for fragrance
in the spiritual fruit of love.

Barely Breathing

Thoughts of you so intense,
I can barely breathe.
I want to be liberated from your hold
and I want to be held.
The complexity of you
is driving me into madness.

I tell myself daily my strength
is greater than your grip.
Yet I still hunger.
You tease me with soft whispers
to my heart.
Do you hear me screaming?
Let me go or love me completely.

Please don't play with me.
I am too old to dance to chance.
I need an honest touch
and an outstretched hand.
Can you feel my
thousand pleas for love?

A Friend's Chest

These woods will tear you apart
even if your soul is sheltered
in sacred light.

A divine seed penetrates the womb
and love will burn like a forest fire
spreading pure ash even if
your mind tries on rejection.

From the sacred space in your body
a delicate flower blooms
ready to embrace eternal love.

The power of love against
a friend's chest cannot be denied.
Come into the woods and submit.

Hold Me

You make love to me with words.
I want to taste them forever
and imagine you in my arms.

To physically touch
may be disappointing.
Your words go far beyond
the earth plane where I float
daily in my dreams.

I come to the river of ecstasy
to bathe in love.
You pour the water of delight
over my shoulders.
I curl into ecstatic bliss
screaming deep inside
where no one hears my joy.

There you make love
to my spirit creating
a causal drip of elixir
down my thighs.
My light body bursts
into a waterfall.

Let me go please.
No, just hold me forever.

When You Are Ready

Your touch is holy.
My body is divine.
How can we join
when your emotions are stained
and your mind confused.

Come to the lake.
Sit with divine inspiration.
Let the water massage your delicacy.

Here at the lake you
may find divine ecstasy
when you are ready to let go.

Do not come and insult the water,
if you are not ready to swim with love.

Safe Distance

I have been told the shadows
between your breast are healing.
I want to go there to feel the powerful
warmth of your hold on me.

I surrender. Take me at will.
I cannot resist.
My body aches for your touch.
My mind tries to run away.

My soul resists. It knows
you are the forbidden precious
stone of love I cannot have.

I dream and hope someday you
will walk boldly into my arms
and make every part of me scream.

Then there are days,
I wish you would let me go
so I may move on to heal
in another meadow.

You are beautiful and dangerous.
I love you but you are a divine spark
that has to be free.

Let me learn to love you
at a distance
safe for you and me.

Beloved's Touch

Some days my feelings are fragile.
My heart is tender.
My tears beat against stone.

Tenderness is a real flower
always available for me
and compassion runs down my side

looking for a place to land.
I wander in the forest of life
looking for you.

Desperate for the touch of grace,
my soul gently says,
purify your thoughts

and the Beloved will touch you.
You will float in harmony forever
on wings of divine love.

Intimate Hold

I have intimate moments
sitting by the river.
The clouds get jealous,
turn gray and threatening.
The river still distracts
with loving caresses.

I look up at the clouds
as they hold back tears.
What stories of suffering
do they shelter as the thunder
growls in measured tones.

I want to move,
give the clouds space.
The river won't let me go.

Running Time

My time is running low.
I don't have unlimited hours
to tease you into loving me
and sitting in a false pool.

You tease me just enough
to come back in my mind to you.
Why am I so afraid of you
and keep coming to your space.

I ask my inner self over and over
what do I want from you?
The answer keeps coming back,
enfoldment in your sacred arms.

You are holy filled with grace.
Shame is the shroud I try to release
for pulling you where
you are not ready to go.

Against Her Breast

He lays his head against her breast
and screams silently in water's desire.
He gently wraps his arms around her
desperately trying not to tremble.

The power she holds over his soul
flows down paralyzing his legs.
He wants to touch the diamond goddess
deep within her but cannot move.
He wants to fill his buckets with pieces
of her love to store in his love cave.

Sacred Feminine

The sacred feminine sends the blood
and releases the tension of the Goddess.
When the blood comes,
know that thou art woman
and the womb is sacred.
This portal of holiness is ready
to open and release the blood.

The womb gives birth to
masculine and feminine energy.
We praise the womb for the gift
of the sacred life of flesh, enfolding
soul for a ride on the earth plane.

Only the awakened may touch
the thighs of the sacred feminine
and experience the elixir
of ecstatic love.

The well of love goes deep.
We must pass the physical
to reach the ultimate realm
of the ecstatic womb.

Climbing into Ecstasy

She wandered through
the colonies of physical love,
tested the branches of desire.
None held her up.
Her soul cowered in a fetal sadness
she tried to ignore.

Today she finds herself
in the presence of the Beloved
who touches her forefinger.
Her soul steps out of the fetal curl,
moves toward the approaching light.
Her body tries to resist
but the pull of love beyond the physical
is impossible to reject.

The first time her heart
feels the pull of love,
she surrenders.
Her soul floats in love's light
climbing into ecstasy.

May I share my first
Glass of truth with you
I love you
Can you hang with that reality

Teresa E. Gallion

Love
in the Scents of
Nature

I want to merge
With that waterfall
Feel the chill of ecstasy
On my breast

Teresa E. Gallion

I Promise

The soul has tasted your beauty.
I still live in hope for the experience.
I walk with gratitude that you allow
me to be in your presence.

I promise to be a good Steward
and keep your house clean.
The soul knows what I must learn,
to love unconditionally dear nature.

I take a daily walk in beauty
to learn to embrace majesty.
I confess the sin of no guilt
for endless joy and love.

Earth Love Call

Mother earth made love to me.
She kissed my lips with laughter.
She shed tears to soothe my shoulders.
She opened my eyes with a beauty massage.

She allowed her trees to hug me
with unconditional love.
She commanded the clouds
to dance for me to lift my spirits.

On the bank of the river
she held my hand,
giving me courage to let go
and walk in God's house.

Mother earth made love to me.
I stand in reverence before her
as she pours the rain
of rapture over my head.

Winter Miser

Her primal urges howl like a wolf
before the moon. A need to undress,
expose her nakedness to the wind
reveals itself to night.

She wants to make love
to innocence below the stars.
Her mind rotates one orgasm after another.
Passion so intense, wolves answer her lyrics.

Ecstasy from her thighs
flood the winter sky.
She falls in a blanket of wild clouds
exhausted from a flood of rapture.

But her soul, oh my,
runs a marathon across the horizon,
looking for a safe descent.
Daylight breaks. Her feet touch earth.

She walks the Bosque remembering when
the cottonwoods shed their golden hair.
Now they stand naked in a 72 degree winter
flexing 100 year old sexy branches.

Raise her hat, smile humbly, throw a kiss,
she looks forward to spring buds, cotton
flying over the valley, summer green.
God help us the fires are coming.

Naked Moon

A naked moon smiles from an indigo sky
silently watches two hands joined.
Skins glow on two bodies.

A slow turn to face each other
between the shadow light,
palms sweat with nectar's flow.

Green peeps above its blanket of dirt.
Blades of grass taste spring in the air,
eager to chase it in the meadow.

Two bodies respond to the tickling blades,
embrace each other, roll in the grass.
A naked moon smiles fading into dawn.

Come Dance with God

We sit on black granite
listen to bird gossip,
notice ants march close to ground,
watch squirrels do a 100 yard dash.

Wind whispers in the forest,
throws a party with shadow light,
waltzes between trees.

I take my friend's hand
point it toward the light.
Our hearts beat in harmony
with the universe of love.

The tree branches say,
*Come children come
and dance with God.*

The Longing

I am ash blowing in the wind.
Let me swallow the sunset
to feed my garden's delight.

Watch my heartstrings blossom.
Let me transcend physical boundaries
and wrap my dream in royal purple,

place it next to your strong muscles.
The sacred stair case awaits your arrival
to walk with me in infinite beauty.

The highway to the universe is blood red.
Crystal light seeps through crevices
connecting earth to sky.

My lip bleeds from the weight of love.
The clouds are naked and moody tonight
wanting to melt into you.

Holding On

We collide in midair.
I gaze at your form
against evening light.
A rainbow of colors dance,
flirt with your essence.

I drift back to the rain
falling in my dream.
The fire in the hearth
warms my soul.

Floating in night sweat
on my pillow, holding on
to that one sweet
image of you.

Mountain Meadow

I walk with Rumi
in a mountain meadow,
whisper close to his ear,
What is the lesson today?

Let's go touch every flower
singing in the meadow.
I suppress the why
on the tip of my tongue.

The teacher walks ahead of me,
gives each flower a gentle caress.
I follow behind,
touch flowers along the path.

Caught in the ecstatic grandeur
of color bending toward sunlight,
I lose focus on the teacher
sitting next to a bouquet of Aster.

As I trip over a rock,
the teacher breaks my fall,
puts his finger to his lips.
The lesson today is about love.

Postcard from Sherman

The goal today is to pose
in front of the Sherman tree.
A fence protects him from
the onslaught of humanity.

I step up to the fence.
A young man from Boston
tells me to smile, put my hands
on my hips. I follow instructions.

He takes my picture, asks for a hug.
I say yes, kiss him on the cheek.
His girlfriend comes to hug me
and his Grandmother.

Thank you dear forest
for so much love
gathered by this tree
in five sacred minutes.

Sedona Moment

A sacred winged breath rides the wind
with daybreaks morning prayer.
Radiant light kisses red peaks,
warms the shoulders

of mountains and mesas,
exposes the grandeur
of a million years of labor
released from the sea.

My soul burns with gratefulness
as I echo back my morning prayer
to the red rock sanctuary
my eyes behold with reverence.

I struggle to find language
that captures this landscape
as my heart pumps exhilaration
bordering on overdrive.

I cannot tell you there is a vortex.
I am a simple witness to love
that binds me to a visual feast.
I am full and want more.

Water and Love

Approaching the waterfall
the lyrics of the water
invite me to sit.

I am grateful for the break.
Let the wet music
massage my aching lungs.

I hear echoes in the wind
telling my muse,
share these words with the world.

I soak in celestial moisture,
assimilate the sound and light
of liquid in my bones.

I must rest at this altitude.
Then I will give to the seeker
the words of water and love.

Middle of Morning

A flute melody plays in my head
and lingers in my ears.
Under the cottonwood, everything
vibrates in the flow of nature's lyrics.

Something about that sound
makes the Mesa cheer.
I am courting the skirts of love
as I drag my feet in the grass.

The landscape is bulging
with joie de vivre.
The moisture in the air
flows into gentle coolness.

Birds chirp in random circles
around Ghost House courtyard.
The fresh breath of morning
filters sacred life into my lungs.

I want to share this moment with you.
When I wipe joyful tears from my eyes,
I see little pieces of heaven on earth.
This life is one season of many more.

Red Rock Love

Red rock spirals, buttes and mesas
make a call to my soul
of uncontrollable bliss.

Only my awakened spirit
can hold the feelings
as I drop to my knees.
Is this heaven beneath my feet?

High on a drug called landscape,
what can I do but surrender
as my eyes scan the grandeur
of the Beloved's canvas.

Is this real or illusion
teasing my eyelids, arousing my sensors.
This drug called landscape
sings to my life blood.

I cannot resist.
My legs ache with ecstasy.
Let me embrace this red rock Eden
and fall in love again.

Moving On

I will sleep in the Jemez mountains
on Tuesday after the rain massages
the red rock and the sun comes out.

I will rise like a Phoenix on Wednesday
at sunset. My new body will run naked
in the ponderosa forest. The wind will
give strength to every bodily part.

I will lay down to sleep by the largest tree
in the woods. I will rise in the shadow
of morning smelling like vanilla and
butterscotch and hug the ponderosa.

You will regret leaving me by this tree
as that scent will never caress your nose again.
I am free and the trail offers open invitations
for a seeker headed for the open road.

Private Balcony Oregon Coast

A sea gull owns the morning sand,
waves shout at the beach
and lift my gut in ecstasy.

I rise slowly from the soft heaven of sleep
to light, chasing my love notes.
The sea kisses the morning clouds,
eternity rolls out the white caps of waves.

Today I am in love with the sea.
Let me drink the morning, inhale the sunrise,
bend my knees in thanksgiving.

The light of the universe falls upon my breast.
I am in that space between ecstasy and reverie
where I surrender to feelings
that make me sing and dance.

Everywhere I turn, grandeur surrounds me.
I cannot capture what my eyes behold
and my heart feels.
Just smile.

Today's Fruit

I go to my cathedral
for prayer and contemplation
under the tall pines.

The sweet-scented ponderosa
always open their arms
and smile at me.

Unconditional love abounds
in my woods,
the welcome mat always in place.

I know my home is here
as my soul leaps from the body
and dances in the forest.

My body relaxes and heals
from wounds of the day
as the dance intensifies.

Resilience tags my soul
to never give up on myself,
feeds the body with spiritual fruit.

Gathering the Silence

I enter the forest unarmed
surrender to the trail,
arms raised to honor the trees.

A slow stride presses boots
against crackling pine
and the pop of twigs.

An unannounced squirrel
running up the ponderosa,
jaws bloated, gives me pause

to gather the silence
surrounding me
with a love embrace.

A subtle wind whispers,
this is your day
to speak to solitude.

Specialized Gifts

There is something special about
being in the mountains surrounded
by regal peaks, lush valleys and

evergreen forests rolling between.
Your spirit soars below a blue roof
and a circus of cloud teasers.

Your stride up the road, through the
woods or cross a meadow is a spiritual
and peaceful walk in reverence beside

lush berries, leaves and bear grass.
Touching the soft leaves creates an ecstatic
bond of pleasure between you and the leaves.

Approaching the boat that carries me
across Josephine Lake brings a twinkle
to my eyes as I scan 180 degrees of glory.

A large moose takes a casual drink,
ignores all the two-legged creatures
coming to the boat.

I could stay here forever and never be bored
with the scenic landscape that unfolds.
My gratitude jugs overflow into the lake.
I am in love.

Ignited by Love

We can look at the universe
as a positive force or negative spark.
Only positive energy ignited with love
may lead to hearts open to peace.

To love or hate is a daily choice.
How may you find a bouquet of love?
I decide to take a long walk in the desert
seeking an answer to my pondering.

I walk for many days, cross many roads
and waterways. One day I wake up
in the Sahara Desert enchanted
by soft red sand, sink my feet into a warm

toast to a November afternoon and
the Sahara massages feet swollen with pain.
A touch of nature tickles my toes.
Gratitude flows on the sand in soft shadows.

When I finally come to my senses, I realize
the most powerful dream to embrace me
gives a very simple message. Peace comes
when you surrender to the flame of love.

Wisdom Shares

Thoughts and memory hike in the forest
gather nutrition for the trees.
When evening comes wisdom crawls
with confidence to spiral branches
that reach for the sky.

She tries to hug a Sequoia,
lays her ear against its bark.
It whispers to her,
Someone behind you is admiring your butt.

She laughs out loud as wisdom is shared.
She merges thoughts to
the memory of the sprouts with no time
to engage people watchers.

A young man dances behind her.
He feels the love between her and the tree.
His feet bask in the energy
that floods the ground under his feet.

She hugs the bark tighter.
More people gather around.
Wisdom's nectar makes them dance.

The tree and the girl smile at each other.
They know love is a beautiful place
that can make anybody bend their knees.

Lift Off

Love walks in the flame.
Fan the flame to keep love
engaged in its ritual dance
as you melt in my arms.

I am love filled with you.
A burning, seeking desire
reaches for a glimpse of stars
to lift us into the cosmos.

I want to touch you forever
as your heart flutters in love's light.
Your presence serenades my soul,
moves me with your radiance.

I want to hug the universe,
as a ritual of thanksgiving.
The Beloved's presence gives my feet
courage to face the battering wind.

Emergency

I hold the earth against my breast
and rock her gently with love.
The heat of this union causes
sacred water beads to roll
down my brow.
My body sweats in the name of love.

Come compassionate humans.
Help me console mother earth.
She is in need of our embrace.
Like an angry child's plea,
she calls out for love.

She keeps trying to get our attention
with fires, tsunamis and hurricanes.
We do not listen nor hear her.
How far must she bend our will
before we answer her call to love.

Emergency
9-1-1
This is a call for love.
My name is Mother Earth.

Love
in the Middle of
Grief

He let go of conditions
Loved her without expectations
Touched her with Divine energy
And watched her blossom

Teresa E. Gallion

Mom and Pops

I cruise by the house
to eat Mom's cooking.
She is happy beyond reason.

From the living room window,
I see him stroke my car windows
with love using the morning paper.
Those windows sparkle, spit shine,
love glittering.

I see Mom out the corner of my eye
with a smile from 7th heaven
watching me watch Pops
as I eat her greens and cornbread.

Pops has magic hands dipped in holiness
and Mom has hands of grace.
You cannot compete
with a love like that.

Crossing Over

The swans are waiting
at the edge of the river.
Such beauty to escort you home.

You linger not eating or drinking.
You need to let go for both of us.
Pops is waiting at the entrance
to the rainbow bridge.
The sparrows are singing your
favorite song.

It's okay to go Mom.
I will heal.
I will go to my therapist
in the woods.
She waits patiently for me.

The woods knew you were leaving.
Sheltered me from the grief to come.
But I knew and digested daily denial
because of a weakness to surrender
deep inside me.
Spirit holds me close until
I can let go.

My joy is resting in the storage
room of my heart respectfully
waiting for me to work through
this grief of your leave.

These tears are sacred.
A mark of deep love, an offering
of 10,000 unspoken words
floating toward you.

Let's imagine that last time
we raced to put our pajamas on.
You tucked me under the blanket,
kissed me on the forehead.
You said, *I love you*
and I said, *I love you too.*
Now I must say,
I bid you adieu my dearest love.

As I Turn

I sleep while night plays ritual games.
Divide and conquer the shadows.
No mercy.
They must be put in their place
perfectly aligned on the road
to protect them from night crawlers.

What do you see lurking in the shadows?

An angel's face scolds my tears.
Laughter points its finger
and says let her go.

No one needs to tell me.
I know the colors of the highway.
Forgiveness is blood red from the cut
across my forehead washing the road clean.

I step in line trailing you.
Following the blue light of love,
you approach the ocean of love and mercy,
turn around,
give me your stern look of love.
You say without words
go back to your earthly home.
As I turn,
you dive into the arms of grace.
I bleed for a hundred days.

I found peace in the arms of the Beloved.
No humans were available
and I wanted to release unforgiving anger.

Teresa E. Gallion

For the Healing

Tell the trees do not drop leaves today.
Tell the wild iris do not lick out their tongues.
Tell the sunflowers do not smile today.
Tell all the flowers do not dance
in the wind today.
Tell the river do not sing today.

Today she comes to us, kneels
before the altar of Mother earth,
eyes swollen with grief,
surrounded by our love.
Give her time to shed
the weight of a broken child.

Do not let the humans
invade her space
for they have abandoned her
and she needs us to heal.

Call all the animals to sit
in reverence on the river bank
to support the healing.

I am the Beloved
covering her in love.
Let all the animals, flowers and trees
sing praise songs for healing.

Out of the light her deliverance comes.
I will be waiting at the top of the hill.

The Butterflies and Hafiz

The butterflies left their homeland,
journeyed to get to me.
They knew I felt abandoned
and heard my plea for love.
They knew I was on the tip
of falling into madness
and had to get my attention
to make me remember I could
walk alone.

They arrived on my windowsill,
tapped gently until
I appeared before them.
Their presence took my smile
to the next level.

I could hear them say in my head
get up, put on your boots
and go walking.
You are a big girl now.
You must walk the road alone.
Just look behind you sometimes
and you will see the butterflies
in a rainbow of love flying behind you.

Then Hafiz appeared as he often does
and said stop weeping girl.
You know you can always depend
on me when you need a friend.
Stop depending on those humans.
They always disappoint.
You must forgive them anyway.
They doing the best they can.

Love-Letter to Mom

My eagle eyes weep today.
Unable to see the sunrise or sunset,
but I know it is there.

I see you on the inner planes
smiling at me saying
without words, *I love you.*
Get up and buckle your shoes.
You have things to do.

I hear you Mama.
I am working on getting up.
I need to flood the river
to relieve my soul of grief.

My guardian is with me.
She always waits on the sideline
to catch me if I fall.

My tears are for you and me.
You are beautiful and free.
I am grateful.

I put my happy charms in storage.
I will pick them up
on my way home from grief
holding my love for you.

The Friend Waits

The river of my mind is flooded with grief.
I tread water on borrowed time.
Karmic coins that were in a trust for me
create a light trail to the distant shore.
The Friend waits with outstretched hands.
She knows I will make it to the shore.

Sea gulls circle the air.
Dolphins swim parallel to me.
A school of fish just beneath me.
Sharks circle the outer rim of light.
Everyone is cheering for me
to make it to the shore.
My spiritual guide swims
a safe distance behind me.

I can hear the Friend in my head say.
I cry with you. The water from our tears
are given to the sea to heal.
Your moist face may lay
tenderly against my heart.
Keep swimming, the Friend waits.

I Am in That Space

I am in that space
where Spirit folds me in her arms
and lifts me up.

I am in that space
where my body floats
in the sacred river
receiving a healing massage.

I am in that space
where love enfolds me
unconditionally.

I am in that space
of weeping for my Mom
as the human in me struggles
to merge with grace.

I am in that space
where I walk with Hafiz
and he makes me laugh
through swollen eyes.

I am in that space
of gratitude and love
in the middle of a pandemic.

I am in that space
where I bow before majesty.
Thank you God
for the gift of love.

Scent of Love

Undress your emotions
Bathe them in this stream
Feel the power of the sacred water
Dress you in love

Teresa E. Gallion

Love
in the Fields of
Awakening

Let us break bread together
In the shadows of light
Then join our fire
To connect with light and love

Teresa E. Gallion

Floating

I live in this wild place
beneath the radar of the Sun King,
dance between the shadows,
rub bone against flesh.

Kernels of life flow free through my veins.
I possess a deluxe grin on my face.
Gratitude blazes across my chest.
I fly on a heatwave of joy.

What more can I tell you,
life is good in this sacred realm
where gardens bloom in my name,
water flows like a boundless river.

There is blood on my hands.
They testify to the thorns
that allow me to caress a rose
in the dawn's early light.

The strain of such beauty
brings tears to my eyes.
Draw near to me friend,
I want to kiss you.

Divine Embrace

I walk in the forest
with music in my boots.
My body dances to the fragrance
of light streams sizzling the ground.

Spill all over me
the burning aroma
of your love, Oh Beloved.
I tremble in your presence

taken by the fiery kiss
of your windy breath.
Kiss me forever,
weaken my knees in joy.

May I touch your hand
to feel your flames
burn my inner self.
Let me lie against this tree,

savor your spicy burn
as it engulfs my heart.
I want to stay high forever
from your divine caress.

Sacred ecstasy is the union I crave.
Listen—birds serenade the forest
in your honor.
Dance with me on this holy ground.

Cut my heart one slice at a time
with your love knife.
Let me bleed joy
in the colors of a rainbow.

Let the soft silence of love
take me from this place
to that walk in infinite grace
holding hands with the Master.

In This Moment

In this moment
the trees sway in the wind,
a tickling love hold rubs
a radiant smile on my face.
Can you see it?

My thoughts are boundless,
heart pumps out of control.
I am floating in the arms
of the Beloved.
Can you see me?

My eyes are locked on
the rainbow in the universe
unable to detach from bliss.
A flute spits love in my honor.
Can you hear it?

I am singing the words,
riding on the breeze,
teasing the clouds on
an ecstatic day in New Mexico.
Can you hear me?

What can I say
to help you understand
my intense energy?
Can you feel it?

Come dear friend, hold my hand.
Love of Spirit flows through me
in this moment.
Can you feel me?

Cherry Thief

Your love is like a prayer
that bends her knees.
She leans in with a sacred chant
that beckons waves of light.

Riding rose beds in clouds
take her to a new future.
She reaches for cumulus
humping a blue sky.

She dreams about her imaginary beau
and their mansion in the sky.
A day is an eternity
in a perfect love bond.

Zeus forms in a cloud,
interrupts her dream,
grabs her with his magic
and steals her cherries.

Confidence

The joy on his face
makes me want to sit
on his chest, raise my head,
sing praise to the blessing of birth.

The leaves flowing from his rack
catch my lyrics in the breeze.
He holds his swords ready to protect me.
I am the queen of his heart.

Today I embrace his physique.
His lips invite me to feel the love
that sparkles in his eyes.
I want to roll across the colors

on his chest, touch his green,
drag my feet in his fiery red,
lay on his purple field,
join his purple to mine.

Touch my wings dear oak
with your white thumbnail.
When I fly away to another season,
the mark of your nail

will be my guide back to you.
I will return to you to rest
on that sacred perch
of joy, peace and love.

Arms of Grace

Evening's dust dissolves her loneliness.
A fertile night sky dances,
flirts with open eyes and melting hearts.

Night rhythms heal everything touched.
She raises her hand,
hopes this is her night to be accepted.

The moment of surrender
makes her feel light,
ready to be held in the arms of grace.

There are no angry shooting stars tonight.
Chances are ripe to be received
on the highway of love.

Sidewalk Teaser

She struts down the main drag
in her jazzy skirt.
His hands, squeaky clean, hide
in his oversize khakis,

where they always go
when excited.
No one could see
those sweaty palms turn red.

She takes a side peep,
catches those hazel eyes
and locks him in her glance.

Water drips from his pockets.
Perhaps love will bloom tonight
along the naked sidewalks.

Phoenix Rising

Her love drips like candlewax,
imprisons his tongue.
She erupts like Mt Vesuvius.
He drinks the heat from her thighs,
wants to be burned over and over.

In flames, he fires up her body
from head to toe.
They engage in a slow burn to ash.
The wind smells the fragrance of unity,
takes those ashes into eternity's nest,
bonds and binds them together.
Two new bodies emerge fresh and new.

Her fingers touch his new lips
and he melts into her arms.
Rain blossoms massage their special parts
as he reforms uplifted in a thrust
that rides like a super nova.

Word Power

When the words flow,
I want to wrap them around you
and let you feel the power of love.

When my words let go
I want to watch you lean on a tree
trembling from the strain of ecstasy.

When you look into my eyes
I want the words to explode
in rainbow colors.

When you reach out to me
I want your hands to catch
an enchanted word brew.

Teresa E. Gallion

Healing Time

I love you but I am not perfect.
You love me but you are not perfect.
Morning light hovers over the wounds
that lie across the bed.

I massage the scars on your belly
with a healing hand.
You massage the scars on my back
with a healing hand.
Slowly we surrender to healing hands.

You do not demand explanations.
I do not demand explanations.
Nurturing old wounds is
the focus of this interaction.

I gaze into the miracle
in your eyes and see a paradise
of thundering waterfalls, a lush
forest surrounding travertine pools,
crystal clear and inviting,
hiding behind a scarred mountain.
You look into the miracle of my eyes
and see a mirrored image.

Another day of healing slowly chisels
away the scars. We are working toward
the same destination, paradise on the
other side of the scarred mountain
filled with the love we are hiding.

Edge of Karma

You drive my thoughts
a thousand miles
to the village you call home.
The temple of my heart
lays wasted in your bed,
digs into your icy blanket,
rides your waves of frost.

I must be dreaming
if I'm here with you
on the edge of freezing.
Your cold embrace
sends sparkling chills up my back.
You are my karmic ritual,
payback for exceeding my budget.

I open humble arms,
welcome the opportunity to be with you.
I must pass all my tests this semester,
learn patience in your winter storm,
tolerance as we work through negative baggage,
endurance as we walk the long road home.

The dream gets better every minute.
I see you lying on my chest
wrapped in my arms.
Fields of iris giggle and flirt
with velvet tongue teasers.

A Poet Teases with Words

And he caresses the metaphors that roll off my tongue

makes a pathway of similes to rub my feet.

I walk slowly into his couplets.

We merge into quatrains,

serenade one another with sonnets

and spend the night in a villanelle.

The sun sings a ballad in our honor.

We step into a cinquain,

dance in a senyru.

A pantoum waits in mornings harbor.

We ride waves of haikus to take us home.

Taste the Moment

Sitting on this lily pad,
you and I open arms
to hug the rushing rain
beading like crystal in your hair.

Rivulets roll down my face.
You kiss a drop of water on my lips,
smile, look through me.
Steam rises from my chest.

You reach out and take it in your hand.
United on a branch of love,
we float in the water of fulfillment.
Hearts roll in a gentle massage.

One body dives into the waterfall
spraying the lily pond.
Everything in the pond is temporary.
We are here to savor the moment.

The wisdom of this pond
flows into us
not as two, but as one
as we discover the heat of love.

Dreamscapes

Today my gratitude spills over
like a waterfall of sweet wine
from vineyards in the Elysian Fields.
The ecstasy is so sweet,

showers flood my eyes.
I want to say thank you
for the gift of love.
No words come from my mouth.

Hafiz approaches giggling and says,
Stop crying girl. Let's dance.
My smile stretches across the sky
as he takes my hand.

We dance until the moon rises.
I lay my head against a butterscotch ponderosa,
watch him slip away in my dreams.
Tomorrow is another day for possibilities.

Hamburger Delight

The meal I eat is hamburger
and sweet potato fries.
The burger fat and juicy,
bread a sweet and tender bond.

We all know sweet potato fries
are orange delight for some.
Smash my bread on that burger,
it bounces back.

I lean back in my sidewalk chair,
smile back at the Rocky Mountains,
breathe deep, lean forward and
bite into that burger.

Juice rolls down my face,
napkin floats toward mouth,
taste buds are thrilled and
my feet dance under the table.

My partner says, *your eyes sparkle.*
I love your joy signs. Let's go for
a love walk after you divulge
the secrets of that burger.

Forgiveness

We walk two miles with silence.
Clouds hug the treetops,
grey veils try to smother you
and I laugh to hide my anger.
The glass of vinegar you fed my garden
causes enduring ripples of broken flowers.

We walk today to seek healing in the forest.
I hesitate to hold your hand as I
question my readiness to forgive.
You stop suddenly and howl at the trees.
The wolves answer back with divine lyrics
to ease your pain. My eyes perk up,
attentive to something bigger than me.

Arms open to wrap you in warmth.
My heart's garden feels the boost of letting go.
Flowers raise their heads like a choir
ready to do a praise song.
Forgiveness flows like a river in us.

New beginnings often run deep in the woods.
The crackle of pine needles is music to silence.
A deer crosses the trail, stops, stares, moves on.
Perhaps we can learn to live without baggage.
What a boost to love that would be.

Convert

We left the city exceeding the speed limit.
She said riding in a car was difficult.
I said, *look at that baby's full diaper*
bounce as Mama chases him.
She said, *did you hear me?*

They need to repaint the yellow lines.
You can always entertain yourself
riding in a car. The light and dark
side passes by your window.

She said, *that may work in the city,*
but what happens when you leave?
Things get much better on the open road.

Cows may be grazing in green meadows.
Flowers may be rushing across a field.
Coyotes may be chasing prairie dogs.
Elk may be showing off their head gear.

There are endless sights along scenic byways.
A rush of trees may cause your heart to skip
a beat or two because your mouth cannot
voice what the eyes see.

Open your mind to the possibility
of joy riding. All it takes is
a shift in attitude where I am going.

She is looking out the window smiling.
The love bond of friendship touched her soul.

Spiritual Reminder

Tears are the rain that washes my space.
They do not come often but when they do,
it rains hard on my soul.

When the sun comes out
all my seedlings produce virgin blossoms
that flirt and sway in my heartfelt garden.
These are the things your gaze brings to me.

Then the wind breaks my heart in pieces,
throws them toward the mountain.
Light guides the pieces as they fall
and land on an aspen leaf in one piece.

Renewed, healed, ready
to embrace love again.
We all need a shakeup sometimes
to remind us who is in charge.

I am a stubborn child
and fall off the wagon daily.
My spiritual guide is always there
laughing on the sideline
carrying my bucket of love.

Turning Point

Enormous cold clutches my heels,
climbs up my legs,
freezes me in place.
I send heat waves of love.
My legs move away from the cold.

The voice of a tragic relationship
runs up my spine,
paralyzes my body.
I relax and let go.
The voice melts in the wind.

A broken shadow stands in my lane
blocks my passage.
I throw a pure kiss of love
into its face.
The shadow falls off my path.

The face of lust staggers behind me
reaches for my tail.
I drop rose petals on my footprints.
Lust dissolves into a stream of love.

I walk alone on my trail,
come face to face with fear.
It reaches for me with bloody hands.
I touch the hand of fear
with the light of love.
Fear turns into my spiritual guide.

Come Friend

I am lifted from earthly illusions.
Now seated in the living room
of Divine Love,
my third eye sees infinite beauty.

Lay your head against my chest.
My body will link you to the Beloved.
Touch my smile and see spiritual light.
A seat at the table of love
is reserved for you.

I am here to show you the way.
Don't be afraid.
My touch is honest.
Come, come my friend
and join me at the table.

My Ink Spills

My ink is wine spilling across the page.
The white space is drinking its fill
of sweetness sharing from page to page.
That's like paying it forward in love notes
to the next soul in need of care.

The papyrus is waiting in the corner
to receive the bleed.
I could write for days and still not find
the end of my love for you.

My brainwaves reach for madness
waiting for your touch
in a sweet embrace.

Ways of Love

I love you for the simple things.

The way you say good morning

The way you smile at me

The way you hug with tenderness

The way you look at me

The way you listen to me

The way you encourage me

Are you full yet

or should I continue?

Morning has broken
With seeds of love
Spread across the valley
For beautiful souls like you

Teresa E. Gallion

Epilogue

about the $\mathcal{A}$uthor . . .

Teresa E. Gallion was born in Shreveport, Louisiana and moved to Illinois at the age of 15. She completed her undergraduate training at the University of Illinois Chicago and received her master's degree in Psychology from Bowling Green State University in Ohio. She retired from New Mexico state government in 2012.

She moved to New Mexico in 1987. While writing sporadically for many years, in 1998 she started reading her work in the local Albuquerque poetry community. She has been a featured reader at local coffee houses, bookstores, art galleries, museums, libraries, Outpost Performance Space, the Route 66 Festival in 2001 and the State of Oklahoma's Poetry Festival in Cheyenne, Oklahoma in 2004.

Teresa's work is published in numerous Journals and anthologies. She has two CDs: *On the Wings of the Wind* and *Poems from Chasing Light*. She has published three books: *Walking Sacred Ground, Contemplation in the High Desert* and *Chasing Light*.

Chasing Light was a finalist in the 2013 New Mexico/Arizona Book Awards.

The surreal high desert landscape and her personal spiritual journey influence the writing of this New Mexico poet. When she is not writing, she is committed to hiking the enchanted landscapes of New Mexico and traveling the world.

You may preview her work at

http://teresagallion.yolasite.com

about the Artist . . .

Denise Weaver Ross is an artist, illustrator, muralist and poet who has worked and lived in Albuquerque, New Mexico since 1996. She enjoys collaborating with other poets and writers in creating book covers and illustrations. As a fine artist, she explores her understanding of the world through images richly layered with mythological, natural, cultural and historical references. For her, the magic happens when disparate images combine to make a new and unexpected image with layers rich with hidden meaning.

Find out more about her and her work on her website,
deniseweaverross.com,
or follow her on Instagram @DWeaverRoss.

Other Books

by

Teresa E. Gallion

~ * ~

Contemplation in the High Desert

Chasing Light

~ * ~

All volumes are available at :

www.innerchildpress.com/teresa-e-gallion
&
other fine book outlets

Inner Child Press

Inner Child Press is a publishing company founded and operated by writers. Our personal publishing experiences provide us an intimate understanding of the sometimes-daunting challenges writers, new and seasoned may face in the business of publishing and marketing their creative "Written Work".

For more information:

Inner Child Press

www.innerchildpress.com

intouch@innerchildpress.com

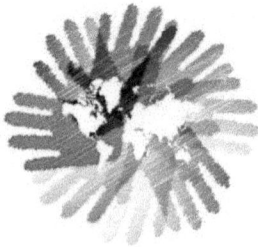

Inner Child Press International

'building bridges of cultural understanding'

202 Wiltree Court, State College, Pennsylvania 16801

www.ingramcontent.com/pod-product-compliance
Lightning Source LLC
Chambersburg PA
CBHW022028090426
42739CB00006BA/327